Great Gifts
Pineapples All Around

(1) 35 cm in diameter. Instructions on page 52.

Festive Flowers

(2) 25 cm in diameter. Instructions on page 75.
(3) 28 cm in diameter. Instructions on page 76.

Simple Elegance

(4) 28.5 cm in diameter. Instructions on page 77.
(5) 27 cm in diameter. Instructions on page 78.

Pineapples Plus

(6) 29 cm in diameter. Instructions on page 79.
(7) 22 cm in diameter. Instructions on page 80.

Pluperfect

(8) 20 cm in diameter. Instructions on page 81.
(9) 23 cm in diameter. Instructions on page 82.

You'll need:
Crochet cotton DMC No. 40, 50g cream (437)
Steel crochet hook:
Crochet hook (0.90 mm)
Finished size:
38 cm in diameter.

38 cm in diameter

Chart on measurement

1 row = 20 loops

180-dc

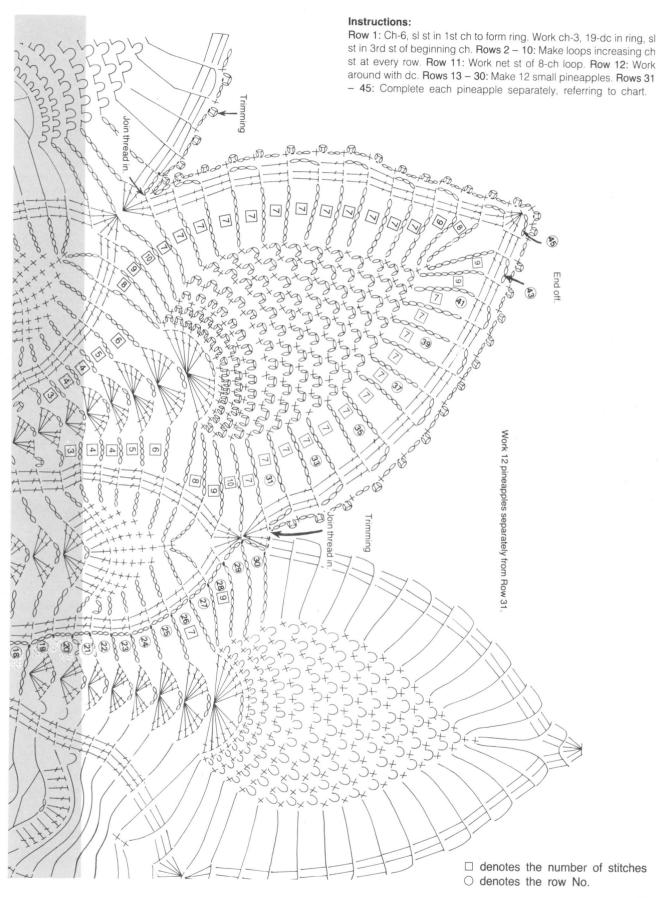

Instructions:

Row 1: Ch-6, sl st in 1st ch to form ring. Work ch-3, 19-dc in ring, sl st in 3rd st of beginning ch. Rows 2 – 10: Make loops increasing ch st at every row. Row 11: Work net st of 8-ch loop. Row 12: Work around with dc. Rows 13 – 30: Make 12 small pineapples. Rows 31 – 45: Complete each pineapple separately, referring to chart.

Work 12 pineapples separately from Row 31.

□ denotes the number of stitches
○ denotes the row No.

Sunshine Still-life

(10) 38 cm in diameter. Instructions on page 12.
(11) 28 cm in diameter. Instructions on page 16.

You'll need:
Crochet cotton DMC No. 40, 30g yellow (743)
Steel crochet hook:
Crochet hook (0.90 mm)
Finished size:
28 cm in diameter.
Instructions:
Row 1: Work ch-9, sep tr and repeat "ch-8, 2-sep tr cluster" 7 times, ch-8, sl st at the end. Row 2: Ch-1 and repeat around "(1-sc, 1-hdc, 1-dc, 1-tr, 1-dtr), ch-5 and steps in (   ) in the other way" 8 times. Row 3: Work sl st until the beginning of ch-5 of the previous row, ch-5 and repeat "ch-1, 1-dtr" 9 times, ch-4. Work dtr instead of first ch-5 from next row. Rows 4 – 10: Make 8 pineapple patterns. Rows 11 – 15: Make other pineapples between small ones (completed at Row 11). Rows 16 – 25: Work fan-shape patterns between pineapples. Row 26: Referring to chart, work around with sc and 3-ch picot and complete.

Shown on page 18.

You'll need:
Crochet cotton DMC No. 40, 5g each of white (801) and pink gradation (776), 10g each of green (913) and green gradation (952).

Steel crochet hook:
Crochet hook (0.90 mm)

Finished size:
21 cm.

Instructions:
Row 1: Work 20-sc to form ring. **Rows 2 – 3:** Work ch-4, 3-tr cluster, "ch-5, 4-tr cluster" 9 times, ch-5 and sl st at the end. **Rows 4 – 6:** Work ch-4 ch-2, 1-tr and repeat "ch-3, 1-tr, ch-2, 1-tr" increasing ch between V-shape on Rows 5 and 6. Join clover leaves together alternating green gradation and green. After finishing leaves, work Row 7 of center motif with sc joining with clover leaves.

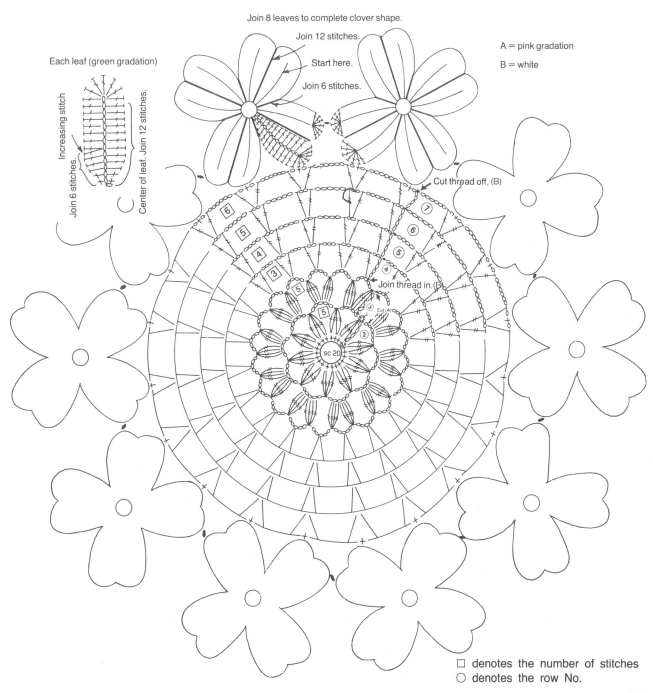

Join 8 leaves to complete clover shape.

Join 12 stitches.

Start here.

Join 6 stitches.

A = pink gradation

B = white

Each leaf (green gradation)

Increasing stitch

Join 6 stitches.

Center of leaf. Join 12 stitches.

Cut thread off. (B)

Join thread in. (B)

Cut (A)

sc 20

□ denotes the number of stitches
○ denotes the row No.

Circles of Delight

(12) 21 cm in diameter. Instructions on page 17.
(13) 34 cm in diameter. Instructions on page 20.

Shown on page 19.

You'll need:
Crochet cotton DMC No. 40. 30g white (801)
Steel crochet hook:
Crochet hook (0.90 mm)
Finished size:
34 cm in diameter.

Instructions:
Row 1: Ch-10, sl st in 1st ch to form ring. Work ch-4, "ch-1, 1-tr" 19 times, ch-1, sl st at the end. Rows 2 – 4: Work tr and picot alternately, increasing ch between sts. Rows 5 – 6: Make petals. Row 7: Work around with tr and picot but making tr and dtr alternately to even sts. Row 8: Work around with tr and picot. Row 9: Work around with tr and ch. Row 10: Make petals. Rows 11 – 12: Work ch and picot around. Work Row 5 of outside motifs, joining with center motif by sl st.

□ denotes the number of stitches
○ denotes the row No.

14

Shown on page 22.

You'll need:
Crochet cotton DMC No. 40, 10g white (801), 5g dark pink (3326), 5g light pink (818).
Steel crochet hook:
Crochet hook (0.90 mm)
Finished size:
22 cm in diameter.
Instructions:
Row 1: Ch-10, sl st in 1st ch to form ring. Work ch-3, 31-dc, sl st in 3rd st of beginning ch. Rows 2 – 8: Work net st of ch-5. Row 9: Work around with 5-dc in each 5-ch loop of previous row (dark pink). Rows 10 – 15: Work net st of ch-5. Row 16: Work sc around, referring to chart (light pink).
Motif — Row 1: Ch-5, sl st in 1st ch to form ring. Work ch-3, "ch-3, 1-dc" 5 times, ch-3 and sl st at the end. Row 2: Ch-1 and repeat "1-sc, 1-hdc, 3-dc, 1-hdc, 1-sc" to make 6 petals. Row 3: Use white thread from Row 1, and work ch-1, "ch-5, 1-sc" 5 times, ch-5 and sl st in 1st ch. Row 4: Work ch-1, "1-sc, 1-hdc, 5-dc, 1-hdc, 1-sc" 6 times. Join 10 each of A and B motifs alternately, working sl st.

Use white thread on Rows 1 and 3 of motif A and B, dark pink on Rows 2 and 4 in motif A, and light pink on that of motif B.

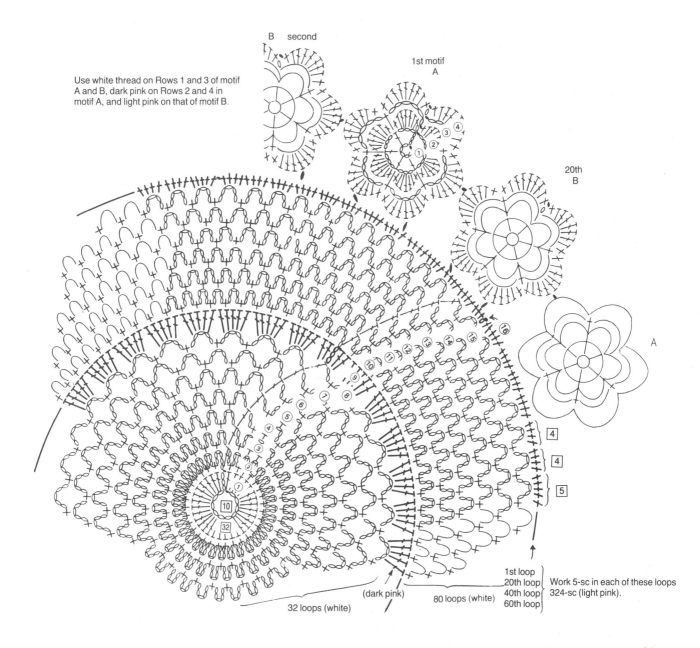

B second

1st motif
A

20th
B

A

1st loop
20th loop
40th loop
60th loop

Work 5-sc in each of these loops 324-sc (light pink).

(dark pink)

80 loops (white)

32 loops (white)

21

A Delightful Duet

(14) 22 cm in diameter. Instructions on page 21.
(15) 37 ch × 19.5 cm. Instructions on page 83.

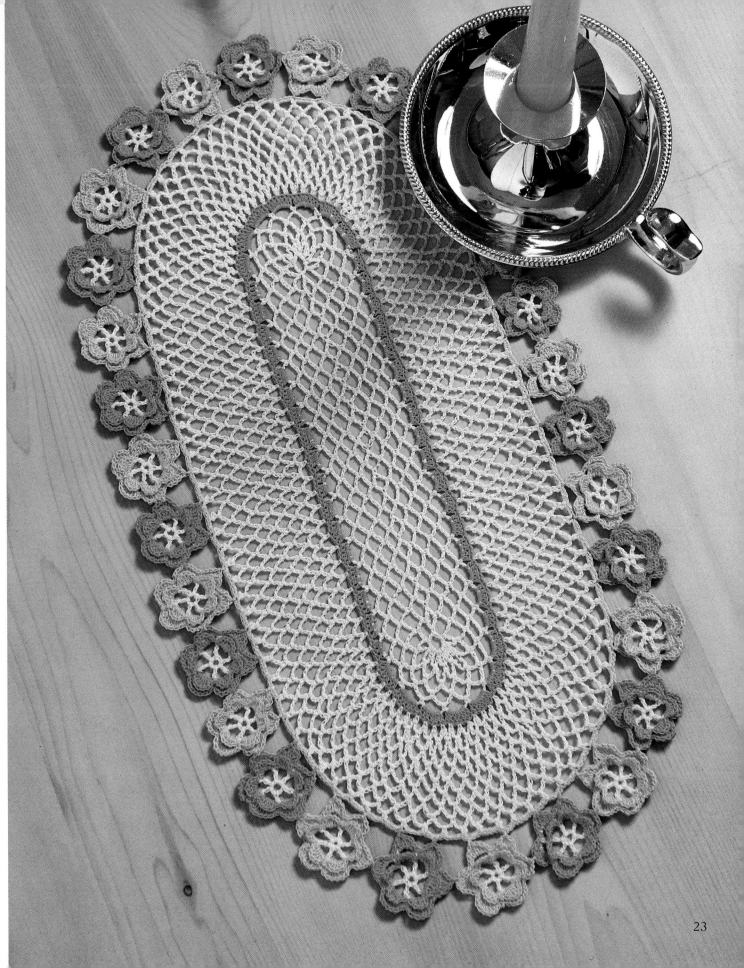

16

You'll need:
Crochet cotton DMC No. 40, 50g white (801)
Steel crochet hook:
Crochet hook (0.90 mm)
Finished size:
53 cm × 34 cm.

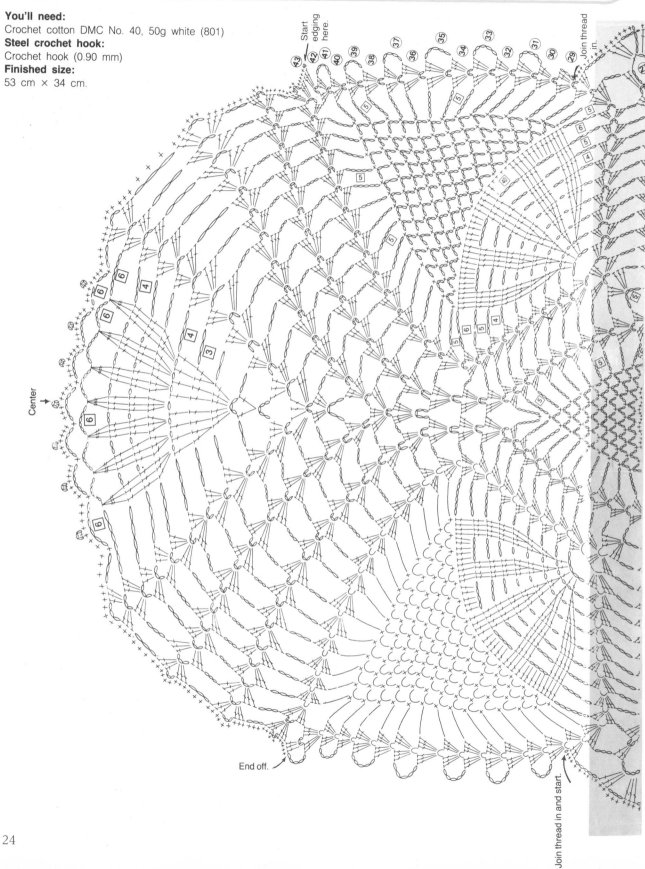

Start edging here.

Join thread in.

Center

End off.

Join thread in and start.

24

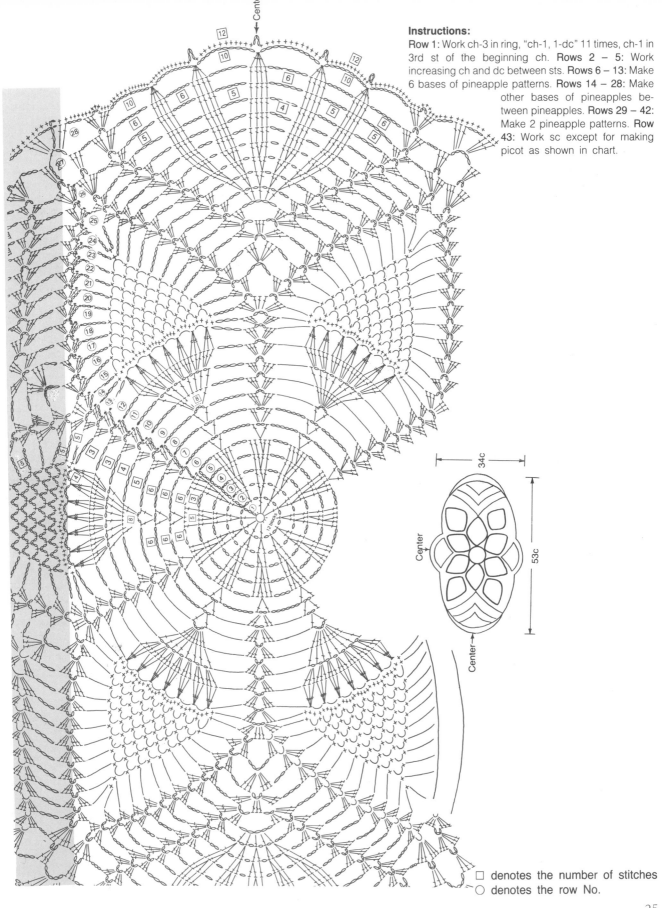

Instructions:
Row 1: Work ch-3 in ring, "ch-1, 1-dc" 11 times, ch-1 in 3rd st of the beginning ch. **Rows 2 – 5:** Work increasing ch and dc between sts. **Rows 6 – 13:** Make 6 bases of pineapple patterns. **Rows 14 – 28:** Make other bases of pineapples between pineapples. **Rows 29 – 42:** Make 2 pineapple patterns. **Row 43:** Work sc except for making picot as shown in chart.

Center

34c

53c

Center

Center

Stunning Elegance

(16) 53 cm × 34 cm. Instructions on page 24.
(17) 40 cm in diameter. Instructions on page 28.

Shown on page 27.

You'll need:
Crochet cotton DMC No. 40, 40g white (801)
Steel crochet hook:
Crochet hook (0.90 mm)
Finished size:
40cm in diameter.

Instructions:
Row 1: Work 16-sc in ring. **Row 2:** Work ch-3, ch-5, "2-dc cluster, ch-5" 7 times, 1-dc, sl st in 3rd st of the beginning ch. **Row 3:** Work sl st until center of ch-5 on previous row. Work ch-1, "1-sc, ch-11" 8 times, sl st in 1st sc. **Rows 4 – 11:** Make 8 bases of pineapples, increasing or decreasing dc and ch between sts. **Rows 12 – 27:** Make 8 pineapple patterns. **Rows 28 – 42:** Make other pineapples between already completed pineapples (up to Row 27).

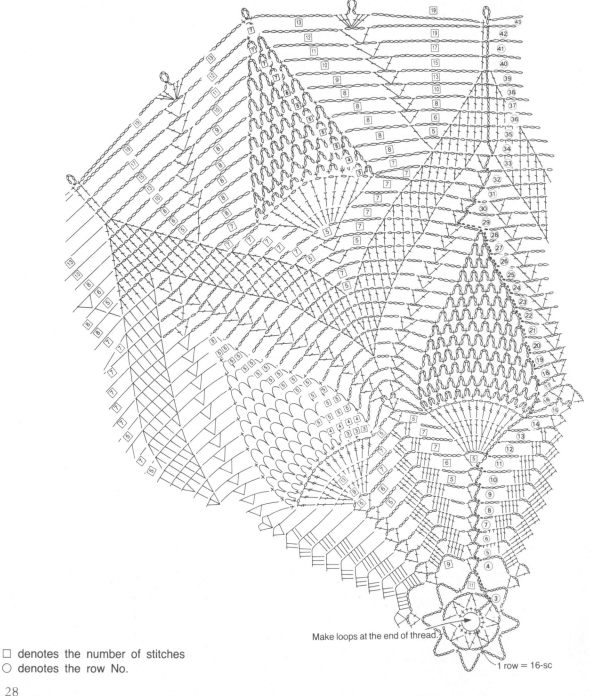

Make loops at the end of thread.

1 row = 16-sc

□ denotes the number of stitches
○ denotes the row No.

Shown on page 30.

You'll need:
Crochet cotton DMC No. 40, 20g white (801)
Steel crochet hook:
Crochet hook (0.90 mm)
Finished size:
30 cm × 22.5 cm.
Instructions:
Motif — Ch-16 in 1st ch to form ring. **Row 1:** Work ch-4, "ch-2, 1-tr," 15 times ch-2. **Row 2:** Ch-1, and repeat "1-sc in tr, 2-sc in loop of previous row". **Row 3:** Repeat from around with 4-qtr cluster in 4-sc

of previous row, ch-13 (except ch-7 at the beginning of the row).
Row 4: Work ch-1, 13-sc in 13-ch loop of previous row.
Joining — From second motif, join to next motif at the center of 13-sc on Row 4 by working sl st. First, join 4 motifs and make piece in the center. Then join two more motifs and make another piece. Work in same way to enlarge. Join 12 motifs 4 by 3 to complete.
Piece — Ch-14 in 1st ch to form ring. **Row 1:** Ch-1, 16-sc in ring. **Row 2:** Ch-1, "1-sc in sc of previous row, ch-11 and skip 3-sc" 4 times. **Row 3:** Ch-1, work 11-sc in loop of previous row, joining with motifs at the center of 11-sc by sl st. Make pieces between motifs.

18

Placemats with Pizazz

(18) 30 cm × 22.5 cm. Instructions on page 29.
(19) 42 cm × 27 cm. Instructions on page 32.

19

You'll need:
Crochet cotton DMC No. 40, 50g white (801)
Steel crochet hook:
Crochet hook (0.90 mm)
Finished size:
42 cm × 27 cm
Instructions:
Motif — Ch-12 in 1st ch to form ring. **Row 1:** Ch-1, 2-sc in ring. **Row 2:** Work "2-tr cluster, (except ch-4 at the beginning of the row) ch-6, 3-tr puff, ch-6" 4 times. **Row 3:** Work "<4-dc in 6-ch loop of previous row (except ch-3 at the beginning of the row)>, ch-6, steps in < > once, ch-2" 4 times.

Joining — From second motif, join together on Row 3 by working sl st. There are two ways to join the corner of motifs. Join from second motif at the point gathering 2 corners, and from 4th motif at the point gathering 4 corners drawing 3 loops together.

Edging — Join thread at the corner and work with ch-4, 2-tr cluster, 5-ch picot, "(ch-4, 3-tr cluster, 5-ch picot) 2 times, 3-tr cluster." Then repeat steps in " " 3 times and 3-tr cluster alternately at the sides, and work steps in " " 8 times at the corners.

Chart on measurement

Joining motifs

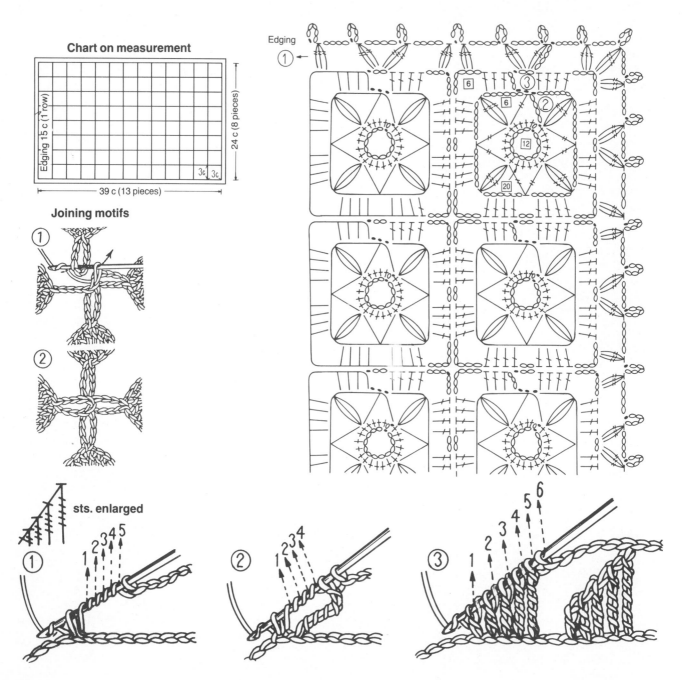

sts. enlarged

You'll need:
Crochet cotton DMC No. 40, 20: 30g each of ivory (ecru nat.), blue (334), green gradation (954). 21: 10g sky blue (800). 22: 20g white (801). 23: 10g sky blue (334). Each cloth 35 cm × 30 cm.
Steel crochet hook:
Crochet hook (0.90 mm)
Finished size:
20 41 cm × 36 cm. 21 37 cm × 32 cm.
22 38 cm × 33 cm. 23 38 cm × 33 cm.
Instructions:
Make each cloth the same size: Cut out the cloths with 0.5 cm hem allowance. Fold the hem twice and tack.

20: Work 1-sc, ch-1 alternately wrapping up the hem. Work 25 sts in 1 pattern and make 11 by 6 patterns. Work corners referring to chart.
21: Make sts as for 20. **Rows 2 – 4:** Work net st of ch-4. Make patterns on Row 5 working one pattern in two loops. Make 31 by 21 patterns and work corners referring to chart.
22: Make sts as for 20. **Row 2:** Work around with ch-5, 1-sc. **Row 3:** Work 1-dtr, ch-5 around. **Row 4:** Work 2-dc cluster, ch-6. **Row 5:** Work sc, sl st-picot. Work 16 sts in 1 pattern and make 14 by 10 patterns. Work corners referring to chart.
23: Make sts as for 20. Work 8 sts in 1 pattern and make 34 by 19 patterns. Work corners referring to chart.

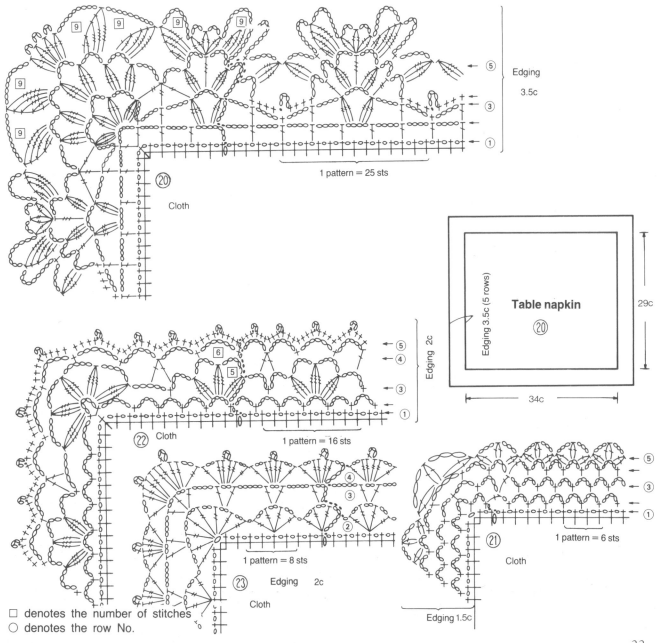

□ denotes the number of stitches
○ denotes the row No.

Great Edgings

20

21

22

23

Nifty Napkins

(20) 41 cm × 36 cm (21) 37 cm × 32 cm (22) (23) 38 cm × 33 cm (24) 48 cm × 34 cm
Instructions on page 33 and 36.

Shown on page 35.

You'll need:
Crochet cotton DMC No. 40, 15g each of yellow (743), ivory (ectu nat.), blue (799), green gradation (952). Cloth 45 cm × 31 cm.
Steel crochet hook:
Crochet hook (0.90 mm)
Finished size:
48 cm × 34 cm.
Instructions:
Cut out the cloths with 0.5 cm folding allowance. Fold the hem twice and tack. Work around with 1-sc, ch-1, making multiple sts of 1 pattern (13 sts). Make 22 by 16 patterns to complete. Work each corner referring to chart.

Table napkin

Edging 2c (4 rows)

30c

44c

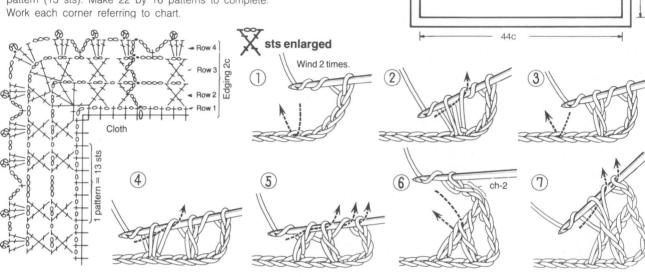

Shown on page 38.

You'll need:
Crochet cotton DMC No. 40, 10g each of Turkish blue (789) and pink (3326). Cloth 22 cm in diameter, two.
Steel crochet hook:
Crochet hook (0.90 mm)
Finished size:
22 cm in diameter.

Instructions:
Ch-304 in 1st ch to form ring. **Row 1:** Work 1-dc in every ch (ch-3 at the beginning of the row). **Rows 2 – 4:** Work 8-dc in 1 pattern and make 38 patterns.
Finishing — Cut cloths 20 cm in diameter. Place lace 1 cm in from edge. Stitch with same colored thread, fold the hem back 0.5 cm, and stitch.

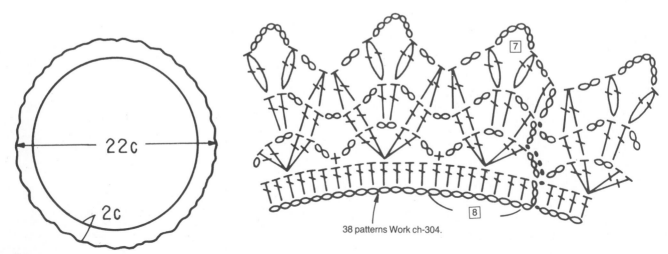

38 patterns Work ch-304.

Continued from page 41

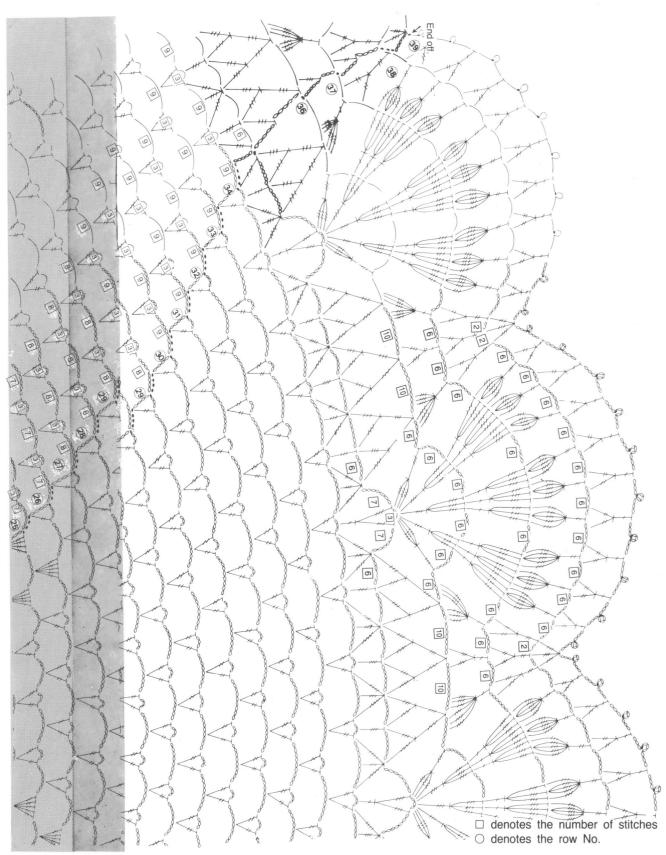

End off.

□ denotes the number of stitches
○ denotes the row No.

A Doily Starburst

(25) 22 cm in diameter. Instructions on page 36.
(26) 35 cm in diameter. Instructions on page 44.

① These show the number of times to wind up (4 times).

② These show the number of times to pull out (2 times).

③ Then, these show the number of more times to wind up (2 times).

How to work inverted Y-shape stitch

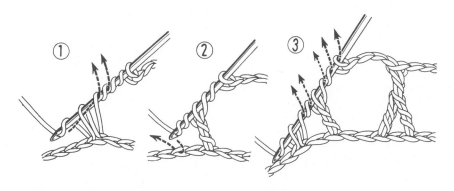

① Wind thread 4 times and pull 2 sts out together 2 times from top of the hook.
② Then, wind 2 more times, holding sts on the hook, and pull thread out from alternate st.
③ Pull out as shown to complete st.

Wind thread 6 times and pull 2 sts out together 3 times. Then, wind 3 more times and make unfinished 3-dtr st by st. Draw 5 sts at a time and then pull 2 sts out together 3 times.

Work same as for inverted Y-shape stitch, except for working unfinished 3-dtr in 1 st.

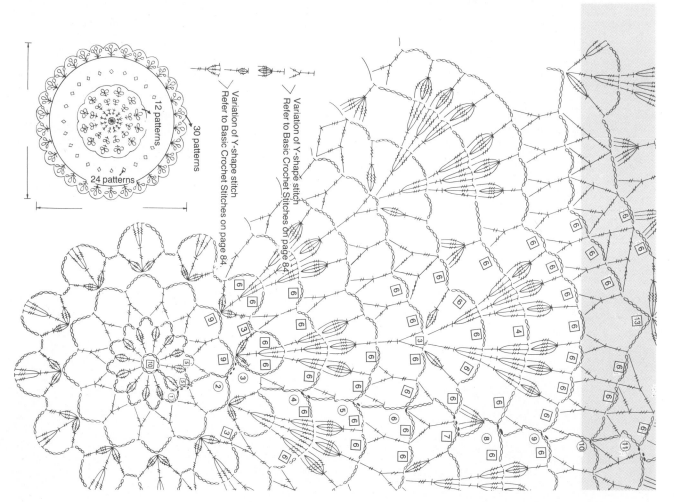

12 patterns

30 patterns

24 patterns

Variation of Y-shape stitch
Refer to Basic Crochet Stitches on page 84.

Variation of Y-shape stitch
Refer to Basic Crochet Stitches on page 84.

Continued on page 37.

You'll need:
Crochet cotton DMC No. 40, 130g white (801)
Steel crochet hook:
Crochet hook (0.90 mm)
Finished size:
93 cm in diameter.
Instructions:
Row 1: Ch-10 in 1st ch to form ring. Ch-8 and work with "ch-5, variation of Y-shape st" around. **Row 2:** Work with "variation of inverted Y-shape st, ch-9" around. **Row 3:** Work "variation of Y-shape st and inverted Y-shape st." **Row 4:** Ch-4, 1-tr, ch-10 and repeat with "variation of Y-shape st 3, ch-6, 1-tr, ch-6."
Rows 5 – 14: Same as Row 4, work variation of inverted Y- shape st and Y-shape st. **Rows 15 – 34:** Work tr and ch increasing ch. Make patterns on Rows 24 and 25. **Rows 35 – 39:** Make scallop patterns working variation of Y-shape st and inverted Y-shape st. Work picot on Row 39.

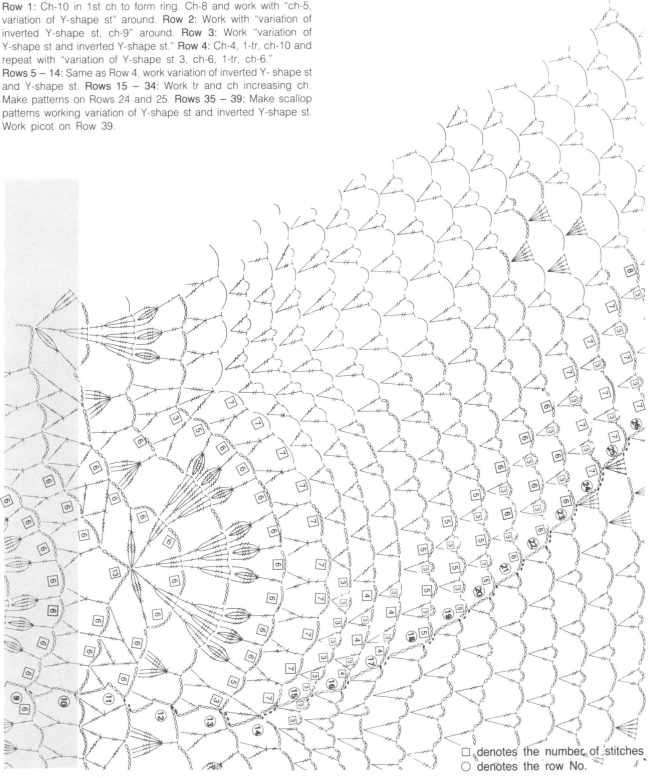

□ denotes the number of stitches
○ denotes the row No.

41

Entertaining Ways with Lace

Centering on Distinction

(27) 93 cm in diameter. Instructions on page 40.

26   Shown on page 39.

You'll need:
Crochet cotton DMC No. 40, 20g white (801) Cloth (natural color)
20.5 cm × 20.5 cm.
Steel crochet hook:
Crochet hook (0.90 mm)
Finished size:
35 cm in diameter.
Instructions:
Ch-264 in 1st ch to form ring. **Row 1:** Work 1-dc in each ch (ch-3 at
the beginning of the row). **Rows 2 – 4:** Make 1 pattern in every 4-dc
of previous row and repeat 66 patterns around. Work sc between sc

of previous row on Row 4. **Rows 5 – 7:** 2 patterns of Row 4 become
1 pattern of Row 5 and work 33 patterns around. Increase sts from
Row 6 and 7 to make frill. Work 10-dc in loop of previous row on Row
7. **Rows 8 – 12:** Make 33 frilled- scallop patterns around. Anchor
with 2-tr in same st between 2-dc of previous row on Row 8.
Finishing — Cut out cloth 20.5 cm in diameter. Place lace 1 cm in
from the edge. Tack the hem, shaping in circle. Stitch one ch by one
st with white thread from front side. Turn over and fold the hem back
at almost the top of Row 1 dc and stitch on dc. Take tacks away.
Spray starch and dry, fixing ruffle.

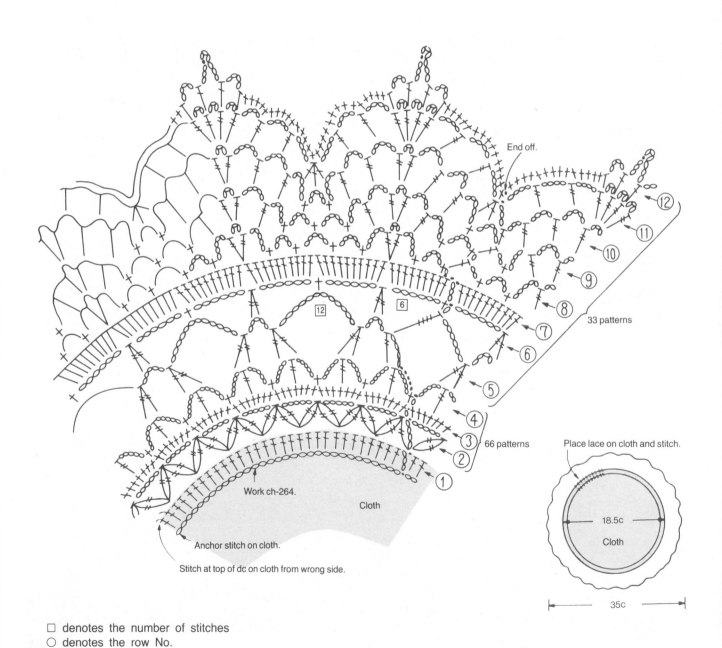

□ denotes the number of stitches
○ denotes the row No.

You'll need:
Crochet cotton No. 40, 150g white (801)
Steel crochet hook:
Crochet hook (0.90 mm)
Finished size:
126 cm × 42 cm (Motif: 10.5-cm square)
Instructions:
Row 1: Make a loop at the end of cotton. Work 16-sc in ring. **Row 2:** Repeat around with "2-tr cluster (work ch-4 at the beginning of the row) ch-7" 8 times. **Row 3:** Sl st on ch-3 of previous row and repeat around with V-shape st <1-dc (ch-3 at the beginning of the row)

ch-3, 1-dc> and ch-3, 7-dc, ch-3 to make 4 patterns. **Rows 4 – 8:** Increase ch between V-shape st to 5 sts on Row 5 to 7 and 7 sts on Row 8 to make corners. Increase ch between 7-dc on Row 3 and work 2-dc cluster and 5-ch loop on Row 7 to 8 to make fan-shape pattern. **Row 9:** Work 2-dc cluster, ch-13 at every corner and work sc-picot with 7-ch (5-ch at the middle) for fan-shape.

Joining — From second motif, join motifs at same point of picot and at the center of 13-ch loop of corner on last row. Make 48 motifs joining 11 by 4. From 2nd to 4th motif, work sl st in 7th ch of 1st motif to join 4 corners.

(28) 126 cm × 42 cm. Instructions on page 45.
(29) 105 cm × 35 cm. Instructions on page 48.

28

29

Shown on page 47.

You'll need:
Crochet cotton DMC No. 40, 120g white (801)
Steel crochet hook:
Crochet hook (0.90 mm)
Finished size:
105 cm × 35 cm
Instructions:
Row 1: Work ch-43 (including ch-3 of the beginning) and repeat "ch-2, 1-dc" to make 13 square mesh. **Rows 2 – 3:** Work ch-3, "ch-2, 1-dc" 6 times, 3-dc and repeat " " 6 times. **Row 4:** Work ch-3,

"ch-2, 1-dc" 4 times, 6-dc, " " once, 6-dc and repeat " " 4 times. **Row 5:** Work ch-3, "ch-2, 1-dc" 3 times, 3-dc, " " once, 3-dc, ch-5, 4-dc, steps in " " once, 3-dc and repeat steps in " " 3 times. **Row 6:** Work ch-3, "ch-2, 1-dc" 3 times, 6-dc, ch-5, 1-sc, ch-5, 7-dc, and repeat steps in " " 3 times. **Row 7:** Work ch-3, "ch-2, 1-dc," 6-dc. " " once, ch-5, 1-sc, ch-5, 1-sc, ch-5, 1-dc, " " once 6-dc, steps in " " once. **Rows 8 – 13:** Work back the same as from Row 6 to 1 to make symmetry. **Row 14:** Work ch-3 and repeat "1-dc, ch-5, 2-dc, ch-3, 1-sc, ch-3, 1-dc." From second motif, work sl st at the point as shown in chart.

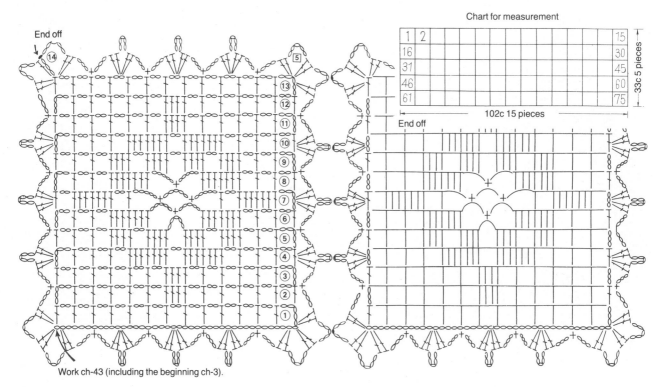

Chart for measurement

1	2													15
16														30
31														45
46														60
61														75

← 102c 15 pieces →

33c 5 pieces

End off

Work ch-43 (including the beginning ch-3).

Joining motifs

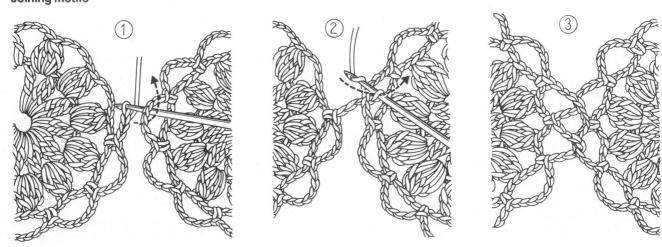

You'll need:
Crochet cotton DMC No. 40, 130g white (801)
Steel crochet hook:
Crochet hook (0.90 mm)
Finished size:
Motif — 8.5 cm in diameter, Centerpiece — 59.5 cm × 42.5 cm,
Chair back — 51 cm × 42.5 cm, Arms — 34 cm × 34 cm.
Instructions:
Motif — **Row 1:** Make ch-9 to form ring. Work ch-4, 23-tr in ring, sl st
in 4th st of the beginning ch. **Row 2:** Work ch-4, "ch-4, 1-tr" 11 times,
ch-4, sl st at the ends. **Row 3:** Work ch-5, 3-dtr, "ch-8, 4-dtr" 11
times, ch-8 sl st at the end. **Row 4:** Work around with "6-dc, ch-3,
6-dc" except working ch-3 at the beginning of the row. Make pieces
between motifs.

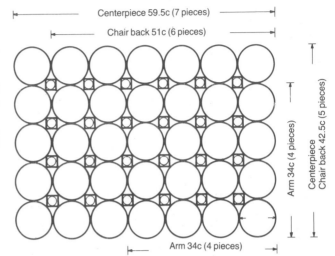

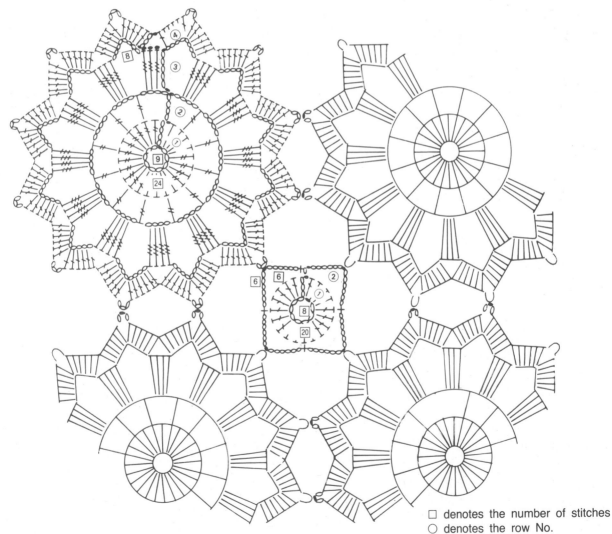

□ denotes the number of stitches
○ denotes the row No.

49

Elegant Ensemble

(30) Centerpiece 59.5 cm × 42.5 cm. Arms 34 cm × 34 cm. Chair back 51 cm × 42.5 cm. Instructions on page 49.

1

Shown on page 3.

You'll need:
Crochet cotton No. 40, 30g white (801)
Steel crochet hook:
Crochet hook (0.90 mm)
Finished size:
35 cm in diameter.

Instructions:
Row 1: Make ch-12 to form ring. Work ch-5, "ch-3, 1-dtr" 23 times, ch-1, 1-hdc at the end. **Rows 2 – 7:** Work net st increasing ch. **Rows 8 – 13:** Work sc-picot. **Row 14:** Work with ch-3, 1-dc, ch-2, 2-dc, "ch-7, 2-dc, ch-5, 2-dc, ch-7, 2-dc, ch-2, 2-dc" 11 times, ch-7, 2-dc, ch-5, 2-dc, ch-7, sl st at the end. **Rows 15 – 21:** Make 12 pineapple patterns. **Rows 22 – 27:** Make fan-shape patterns working pineapples. **Row 28:** Work 1-sc and repeat "ch-6, sc-picot with 4-ch, ch-7, 1-sc in ch-4 of previous row" around and sl st to end.

sc-picot

①

②

③

□ denotes the number of stitches
○ denotes the row No.

52

24 loops

You'll need:
Crochet cotton No. 40, 210g White (801)
Steel crochet hook:
Crochet hook (0.90 mm)
Finished size:
Motif — 11 cm in diameter. Centerpiece — 73cm × 40 cm. Chair back — 62 cm × 40 cm. Arms — 40 cm × 40 cm.
Instructions:
Motif — **Row 1**: Work ch-3 in ring, "ch-1, 1-dc" 11 times, ch-1, sl st at the end. **Row 2**: Work ch-3, 1-dc, "ch-2, 2-dc" 11 times, ch-2 and sl st at the end. **Row 3**: Work in same manner increasing ch and dc. **Rows 4 – 5**: Work with ch and sc around. **Rows 6 – 10**: Make patterns with ch and dc. From second motif, join motif with sl st on the last row, as shown in chart. Make pieces A, B, and C referring to chart and work 4 rows of edging to complete.

Chart for measurement

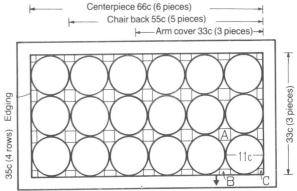

Victorian Medley

(31) Centerpiece 73 cm × 40 cm. Arms 40 cm × 40 cm. Chair back 62 cm × 40 cm. Instructions on page 53.
(32) 95 cm × 75 cm. Instructions on page 56.

31

Shown on page 55.

You'll need:
Crochet cotton DMC No. 40, 200g white (801)
Steel crochet hook:
Crochet hook (0.90 mm)
Finished size:
95 cm × 75 cm (each motif: 10-cm square).

Instructions:
Row 1: Make ch-8 to form ring. Work ch-1, "3-sc, ch-3" 4 times, sl st at the end. **Row 2**: Work 4 sl st on previous row as shown, and repeat around with "9-tr, ch-3" except working ch-3 at the beginning of row. **Row 3**: Work ch-1 "1-sc, ch-2, 1-dc, ch-2, 1-dc, ch-2" 4 times, sl st in 1st ch. **Row 4**: Work sl st in sc of previous row. Repeat "7-sc, (ch-2, 2-dc) 3 times, ch-2" around. **Rows 5 – 10**: Complete 4 pineapple patterns. From second motif, join motif with sc on sides and with sl st at every corner. Work 2 rows with net st for edging. Join motifs 9 by 7.

□ denotes the number of stitches
○ denotes the row No.

Shown on page 58.

You'll need:
Crochet cotton DMC No. 40, 60g beige (960)
Steel crochet hook:
Crochet hook (0.90 mm)
Finished size:
50 cm × 38 cm
Instructions:
Row 1: Make ch-16 to form ring. Work ch-4, 6-tr "ch-3, 7-tr" 3 times, ch-3, sl st at the end. **Row 2**: Work around with ch-1 between tr and ch-5 on ch-3 of previous row. **Rows 3 – 6**: Work st with 4 pineapple patterns. **Rows 7 – 12**: Make 8 more pineapples at 4 corners between 4 pineapples. From second motif, join motif with sl st. For edging, work 2 rows of 9-ch loops and repeat around with sc and picot on the last row.

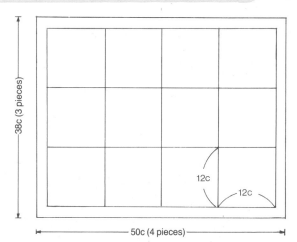

Cut thread off.

Capital Good Looks

(33) 50 cm × 38 cm. Instructions on page 57. (34) 70 cm × 39 cm. Instructions on page 60.

You'll need:
Crochet cotton DMC No. 40, 80g white (801)
Steel crochet hook:
Crochet hook (0.90 mm)
Finished size:
70 cm × 39 cm.

Instructions:
Motif — **Row 1:** Ch-8 to form ring. Work ch-4, 1-tr, "ch-3, 2-tr puff" 7 times, ch-3, sl st at the end. **Row 2:** Work sl st until the center of ch-3 of previous row, ch-4," sl st-picot with 3-ch, ch-5, 1-tr" 7 times, sl st picot with 3-ch, ch-2, tr at the end. **Row 3:** Ch-4, "ch-8, 1-tr" 7 times, ch-8, sl st at the end. **Row 4:** Work around with variation of Y-shape st and triangle st. **Row 5:** Make 4 corners to form square motif. Join 28 motifs and work sc on the first row of edging

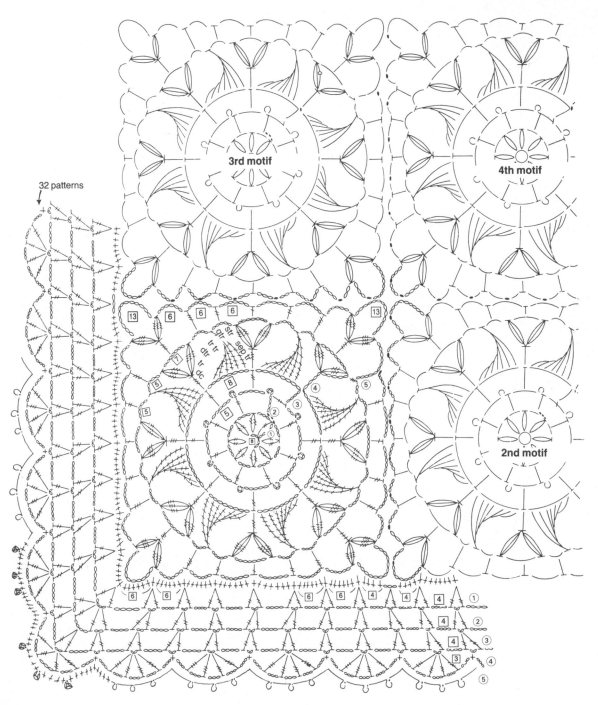

35

Shown on page 62.

You'll need:
Crochet cotton DMC No. 18, 220g, white (5200)
Steel crochet hook:
Crochet hook (1.75 mm)
Finished size:
70 cm × 48 cm.
Instructions:
Row 1: Make ch-8 to form ring. Work ch-1, 16-sc in ring. **Row 2:** Ch-3, "ch-1, 1-dc" 15 times, ch-1, sl st in 3rd st of beginning ch. **Row 3:** Work ch-4, "ch-5, 1-tr" 15 times, ch-2, 1-dc at the end of row.
Rows 4 – 17: Work around with 4 pineapple patterns making 1 pattern with 4 loops of Row 3. Work with 1-sc, ch-1 at the center part of pineapple on Rows 5 and 6, and 1-sc, ch-2 from Row 7. Increase 2-dc and ch-5 in 1-ch of previous row at every corner.

Joining — From second motif, join with other motif on Row 17. Join motif with dc on sides as shown in chart. After working dc as shown, remove hook from stitch and insert hook in the same point of other motif to pull through the remaining stitch. From 4th motif, draw other 3 loops together at this point, joining 4 corners.

Edging — Join thread in the center of shell st at every corner (A). Join thread in the center of shell st at 6 joining points and work 2 rows (B). Then join thread in the corner and work 4 rows on 4 sides for edging.

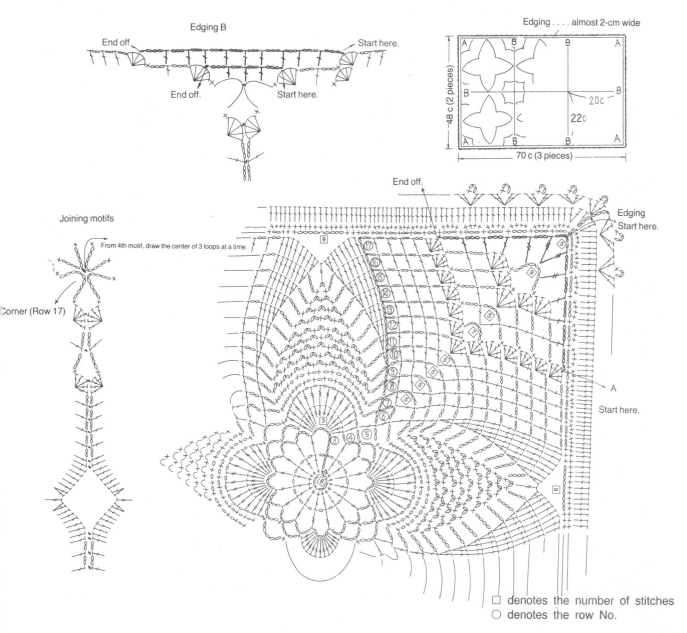

☐ denotes the number of stitches
◯ denotes the row No.

61

Dandy Daisies

(36) 57 cm × 43.5 cm. Instructions on page 64. (35) 70 cm × 48 cm. Instructions on page 61.

35

36

You'll need:
Crochet cotton DMC No. 40, 90 g White (801)
Steel crochet hook:
Crochet hook (0.90 mm)
Finished size:
57 cm × 43.5 cm.
Instructions:
Row 1: Make ch-7 to form ring. Ch-1, 12-sc, sl st at the end. **Row 2:**
Ch-5, "ch-3, 1-tr" 11 times, ch-3, sl st at the end. **Row 3:** Ch-1 and
work around with sc. **Row 4:** Work ch-4, 3-tr cluster and repeat
"ch-6, 4-tr cluster" around. **Rows 5 – 15:** Make 8 petal patterns.

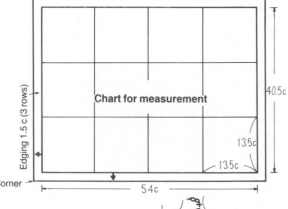

Chart for measurement

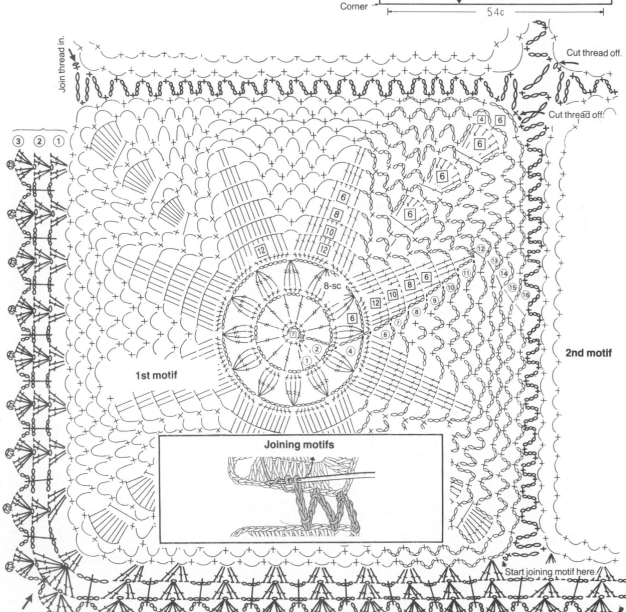

Joining motifs

37

Shown on page 66.

You'll need:
Crochet cotton DMC No. 40, 80g white (801)
Steel crochet hook:
Crochet hook (0.90 mm)
Finished size:
60 cm × 37.5 cm.
Instructions:
From second motif, join with other motifs at the loops on the last row by working sl st. Assemble 40 motifs, referring to chart. To make pieces, work 1-sc, ch-8 in ring and join with motif by sl st and ch-8, sc. Work sl st 3 times to join with each motif.

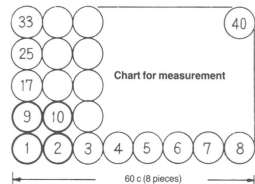

Chart for measurement

37.5 c (5 pieces)

60 c (8 pieces)

□ denotes the number of stitches
○ denotes the row No.

65

(37) 60 cm × 37.5 cm. Instructions on page 65. (38) 52.5 cm × 30 cm. Instructions on page 68.

37

38

Shown on page 67.

You'll need:
Crochet cotton DMC No. 40, 65g white (801)
Steel crochet hook:
Crochet hook (0.90 mm)
Finished size:
52.5 cm × 30 cm.
Instructions:
Row 1: Make ch-10 to form ring. Work ch-4, 2-tr cluster, "ch-6, 3-tr cluster" 9 times, ch-3, dc at the end. **Row 2:** Work around with tr and ch. **Rows 3 – 4:** Work around with 7-ch loop on Row 3 and with 5-ch loop on Row 4. **Row 5:** Ch-3, 1-dc and repeat "ch-2, 2-dc, ch-2, 2-dc" around and sl st at the end. **Row 6:** Ch-1 and repeat "1-sc, 3-dc, ch-3, 3-dc." From second motif, join to other motif at ch-3 by sl st.
Piece — Join with ch and sl st between motifs.

Chart for measurement

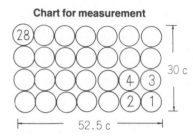

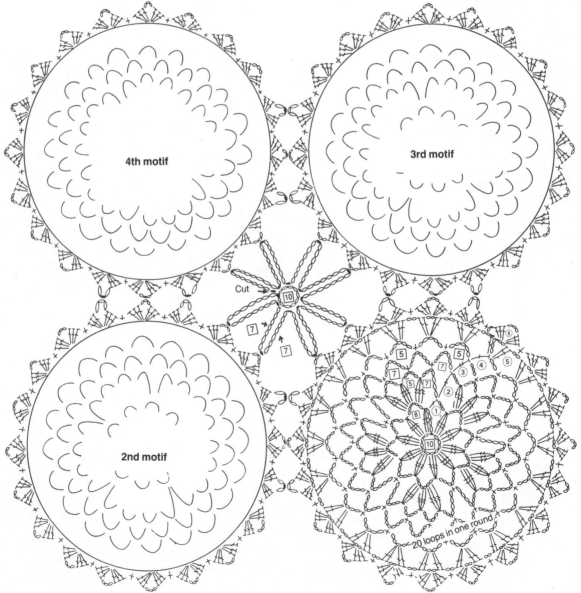

You'll need:
Crochet cotton DMC No. 40, 120g ivory (ecru nat.)
Steel crochet hook:
Crochet hook (0.90 mm)
Finished size:
69 cm × 69 cm.
Instructions:
Motif — Make ch-8 to form ring. **Row 1:** Ch-1, 16-sc in ring. **Row 2:** Work ch-3, "ch-3, 1-dc" 7 times, ch-3, sl st at the end. **Row 3:** Ch-3 and work 47-dc around and sl st at the end. **Row 4:** Ch-1, "ch-22, 21-sc, 5-sc in dc of previous row" 8 times, sl st at the end. **Row 5:** Work ch-3, "12-dc, picot, 3-dc, 3-hdc, 2-sc, picot" and turn back by steps in " " from picot on opposite side. Work dc instead of the beginning ch-3. (Make 8 patterns.)

Piece — **Row 1:** Work 8-sc in ring. **Row 2:** Work Ch-1, "1-sc, ch-8" 7 times, 1-sc, ch-4, tr at the end. **Row 3:** Repeat around with "ch-4, 1-sc, ch-5, 1-sc." **Row 4:** Sl st in 2 ch and work ch and picot joining with sl st at the point as shown in chart. Remember not to work stitches unevenly since there are many spaces in this pattern.

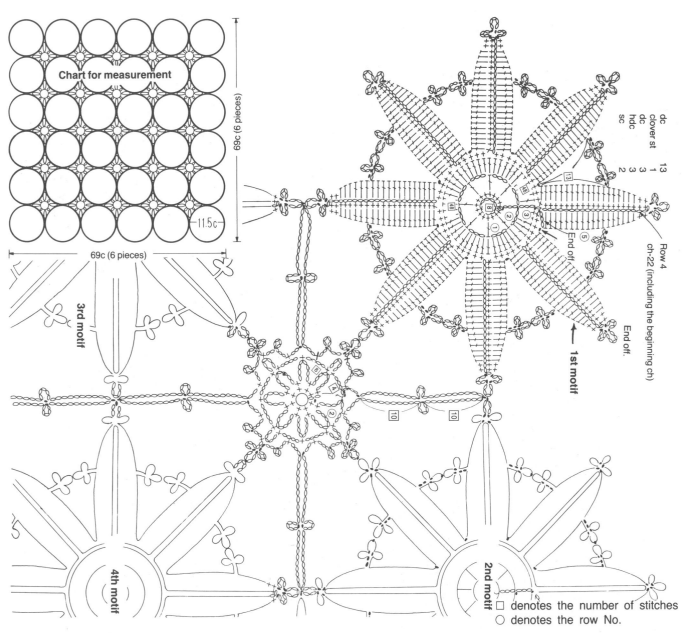

□ denotes the number of stitches
○ denotes the row No.

Beautiful Tabletops

(39) 69 cm × 69 cm. Instructions on page 69. (40) 82.5 cm × 40 cm. Instructions on page 72.

39

40

40

Shown on page 71.

You'll need:
Crochet cotton DMC No. 40, 120g white (801)
Steel Crochet hook:
Crochet hook (0.90 mm)
Finished size:
82.5 cm × 40 cm.
Instructions:
Make ch-10 to form ring. **Row 1:** Ch-3, 23-dc, sl st at the end. **Row 2:** Work ch-1, repeat "1-sc, ch-3" and sl st at the end. **Row 3:** Work sl st until the center of ch-3 and work net st of 5-ch. **Row 4:** Work around with 16-ch loop. **Row 5:** Work around with 3-ch loop. **Rows 6 – 11:** Work plain st with variation of sc separating 6 parts. **Row 12:** Work around with sc and ch to make sts evenly. Make pieces between motifs.

Chart for measurement

40 c

82.5 c

10th motif

11th motif

Join thread in.

Cut thread off

Cut thread off

Join thread in

2nd motif

□ denotes the number of stitches
○ denotes the row No.

You'll need:
Crochet cotton DMC No. 40, 30g white (801), 20g dark blue gradation (823)
Steel crochet hook:
Crochet hook (0.90 mm)
Finished size:
48 cm × 52.5 cm.
Instructions:
Motif — **Row 1**: Work 12-sc in ring. **Row 2**: Work ch-3, 2-dc in 1-sc of previous row. **Row 3**: Make 12 patterns with ch and sl st-picot. **Row 4**: Join other thread in and repeat "1-sc, ch-3" around. **Row 5**: Work around with sc and 5-ch picot. From second motif, join motifs at picot.

Chart for measurement

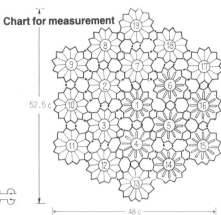

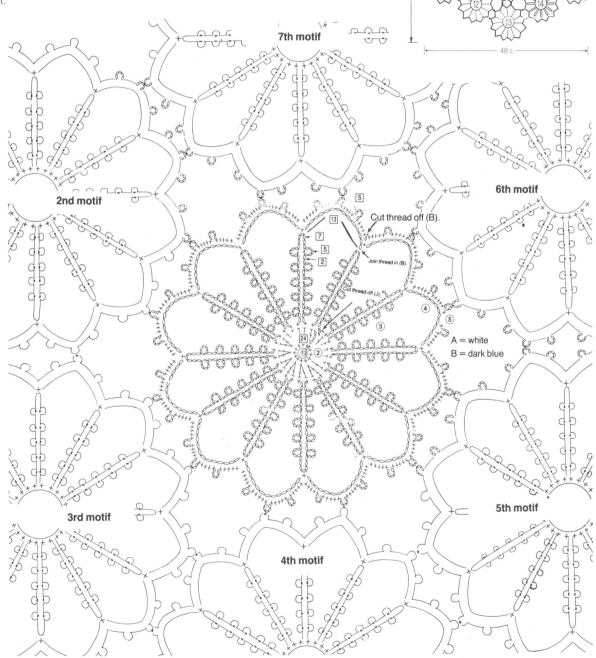

A = white
B = dark blue

Final Word in Elegance:
The Snowflake Centerpiece

(41) 48 cm × 52 cm. Instructions on page 73.

2

You'll need:
Crochet cotton DMC No. 40, 20g white (801)
Steel crochet hook:
Crochet hook (0.90 mm)
Finished size:
25 cm in diameter.
Instructions:
Row 1: Make ch-14 to form ring. Work ch-1, 24-sc in ring. **Row 2:** Work ch-3, "ch-4, 1-dc" 7 times, ch-4, sl st at the end. **Row 3:** Work

ch-3 and ch-1, 1-dc, ch-1, 1-dc, "ch-4, 1-dc, ch-1, 1-dc, ch-1, 1-dc" 7 times, ch-4, sl st at the end. **Rows 4 – 12:** Work in same manner, increasing ch and square mesh. **Rows 13 – 23:** Make new patterns between square mesh patterns. **Row 24:** Work around with sc, making sl st-picot with 6-ch 5 times on each pattern as shown in chart, and make 8 patterns.

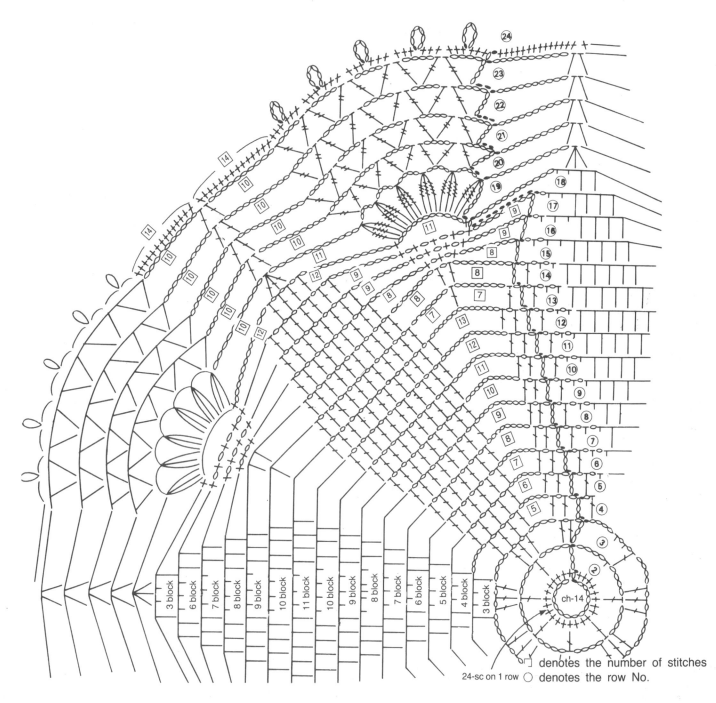

⟨ denotes the number of stitches
24-sc on 1 row ○ denotes the row No.

You'll need:
Crochet cotton DMC No. 40, 20g white (801)
Steel crochet hook:
Crochet hook (0.90 mm)
Finished size:
28 cm in diameter.

Instructions:
Make ch-12 to form ring. **Row 1**: Ch-3, 23-dc in ring. **Row 2**: Work ch-4, ch-2 and repeat "1-tr, ch-2" 23 times and sl st in 4th st of beginning ch. **Rows 3 – 5**: Work sl st in ch-2 of previous row, ch-1 and repeat "1-sc, ch-6" 24 times and sl st in 1st ch. Work same manner as Row 3, increasing ch between loops on Row 4 and 5. **Row 6**: Work sl st in ch-4 of previous row, ch-5, 2-dtr and repeat "ch-2, 3-dtr" around. **Row 7**: Work sc in every st of previous row. **Rows 8 – 25**: Make 12 patterns.

You'll need:
Crochet cotton DMC No. 40, 20g White (801)
Steel crochet hook:
Crochet hook (0.90 mm)
Finished size:
28.5 cm in diameter.
Instructions:
Row 1: Make ch-10 to form ring. Ch-3, 23-dc, sl st at the end. **Row 2:** Work ch-3 and repeat "ch-4, 1-dc" 7 times, ch-4, sl st at the end. **Row 3:** Ch-3 and repeat "ch-4, 1-dc, ch-1, 1-dc, ch-1, 1-dc" 7 times and ch-4, 1-dc, ch-1, 1-dc, ch-1, sl st at the end. **Rows 4 – 10:** Work in same manner, increasing ch and square mesh. **Rows 11 – 20:** Skip one block of square mesh to make pattern. **Row 21:** Work sl st in ch-4 of previous row. Ch-3 and repeat with "ch-6, 1-dc, ch-6 (1-dc, ch-1) 8 times, 1-dc, ch-3, steps in ( ) 8 times, 1-dc." **Row 22:** Make other pattern between square mesh working 16-dtr in ch-6 of previous row as shown. **Row 23:** Make petal with tr and ch, and work around with petal and square mesh alternately. **Row 24:** Ch-4 and make petal repeating "ch-3, sl st-picot with 6-ch, ch-3, 1-tr."

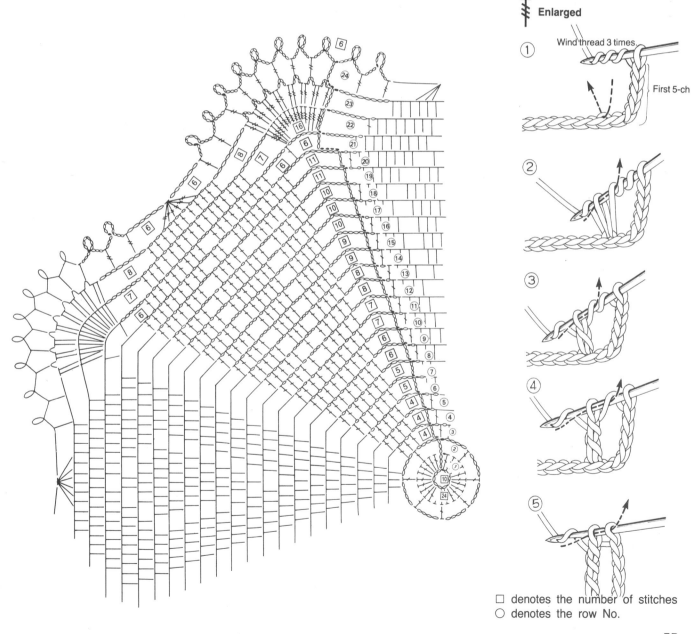

□ denotes the number of stitches
○ denotes the row No.

77

You'll need:
Crochet cotton DMC No. 40, 15g white (801)
Steel crochet hook:
Crochet hook (0.90 mm)
Finished size:
27 cm in diameter.

Instructions:

Row 1: Make ch-12 to form ring. Work ch-15, "ch-3, 1-dtr" 15 times, ch-3, sl st at the end. Row 2: Work ch-5 and repeat with "ch-2, 1-dtr" 31 times and ch-2, sl st at the end. Rows 3 – 4: Work in same manner, increasing ch. Rows 5 – 6: Ch-5 and repeat around with "1-dtr, ch-2, 2-dtr, ch-8, 1-dtr." Increase ch on Row 6. Row 7: Ch-5 and repeat "1-dtr, ch-3, 2-dtr, ch-6 (1-dtr, ch-1) 7 times, 1-dtr, ch-6, 1-dtr." Rows 8 – 13: Make pineapple and fan pattern alternately. Row 14: Work sl st until center of ch-4 of previous row, ch-5 and repeat around with "ch-3, sl st-picot with 6-ch, ch-3, 1-dtr," except working ch-6 and dtr on pineapple.

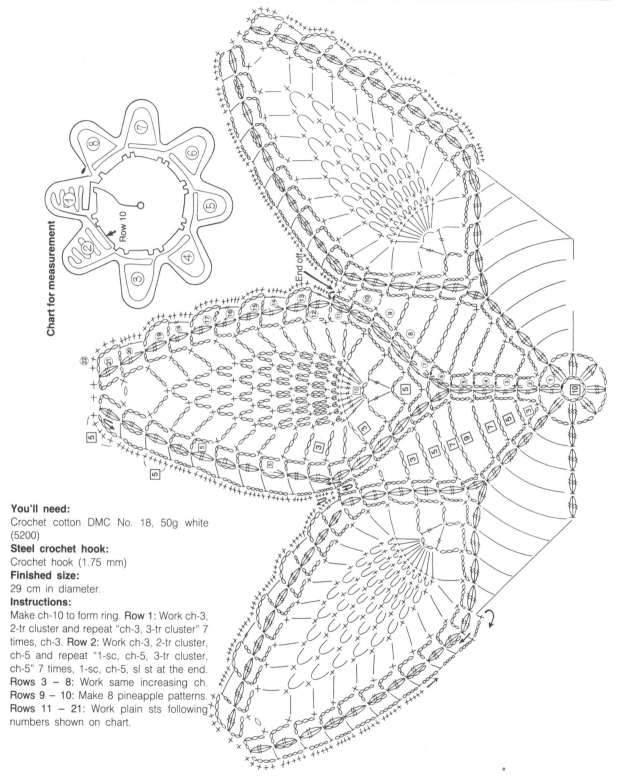

You'll need:
Crochet cotton DMC No. 18, 50g white (5200)

Steel crochet hook:
Crochet hook (1.75 mm)

Finished size:
29 cm in diameter.

Instructions:
Make ch-10 to form ring. **Row 1:** Work ch-3, 2-tr cluster and repeat "ch-3, 3-tr cluster" 7 times, ch-3. **Row 2:** Work ch-3, 2-tr cluster, ch-5 and repeat "1-sc, ch-5, 3-tr cluster, ch-5" 7 times, 1-sc, ch-5, sl st at the end.
Rows 3 – 8: Work same increasing ch.
Rows 9 – 10: Make 8 pineapple patterns.
Rows 11 – 21: Work plain sts following numbers shown on chart.

☐ denotes the number of stitches
○ denotes the row No.

79

You'll need:
Crochet cotton DMC No. 40, 10g white (801)
Steel crochet hook:
Crochet hook (0.90 mm)
Finished size:
22 cm in diameter.
Instructions:
Row 1: Work 16-dc in ring. Row 2: Work ch-3, ch-4 and repeat
"1-dc, ch-4" 7 times, sl st at the end. Row 3: Ch-3 and work around
with 5-dc in ch-4 of previous row and 1-dc in 1-dc. Rows 4 – 12:
Work around with 8 pineapple patterns. Rows 13 – 23: Work
pineapples separately to complete.

Cut thread off.

Join thread in.

Join thread in.

Join thread in.

Join thread in.

Join thread in.

□ denotes the number of stitches
○ denotes the row No.

Continued on page 83.

You'll need:
Crochet cotton DMC No. 40, 15g white (801)
Steel crochet hook:
Crochet hook (0.90 mm)
Finished size:
23 cm in diameter.
Instructions:
Row 1: Work ch-4 in ring and "ch-2, 1-tr" 11 times, ch-2, sl st at the end. **Row 2:** Work ch-3, 2-dc cluster, "ch-3, 3-dc cluster" 11 times,

ch-1 and hdc in 3rd st of beginning ch. **Row 3:** Work ch-3, ch-2, 1-dc, "ch-3, 3-dc cluster, ch-2, 3-dc cluster, ch-3, 1-dc, ch-2, 1-dc" 5 times, ch-3, 3-dc cluster, ch-2, 3-dc cluster, ch-3, sl st at the end. **Row 4:** Work same as Row 3 except increasing ch. **Rows 5 – 11:** Make 6 pineapple patterns. **Row 12 – 19:** Work fan-shape patterns, making pineapples.

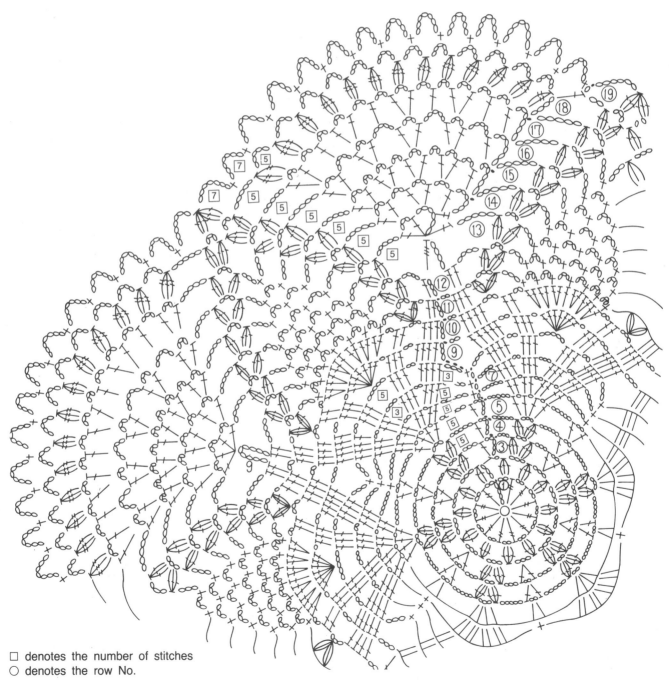

□ denotes the number of stitches
○ denotes the row No.

82

You'll need:
Crochet cotton DMC No. 40, 15g white (801), 8g Turkish blue (798), 6g sky blue (800)
Steel crochet hook:
Crochet hook (0.90 mm)
Finished size:
37 cm × 19.5 cm.
Instructions:
Row 1: Work ch-5, 1-dtr to make 18 rings with white thread, following chart. Row 2 – 6: Work net st with white in 5-ch loop. Row 7: Work around with Turkish blue in dc. Rows 8 – 16: Work net st with white in 5-ch loop. Row 17: Work around in sc with sky blue.
Flower motif — Row 1: Using white, make ch-5 to form ring and ch-3, "ch-3, 1-dc" 5 times, ch-3, sl st at the end. Row 2: Using colored thread, make petals. Row 3: Work sts on Row 1 pulling petals down to the front side. Row 4: Join with the base by sl st, working petal with colored thread.

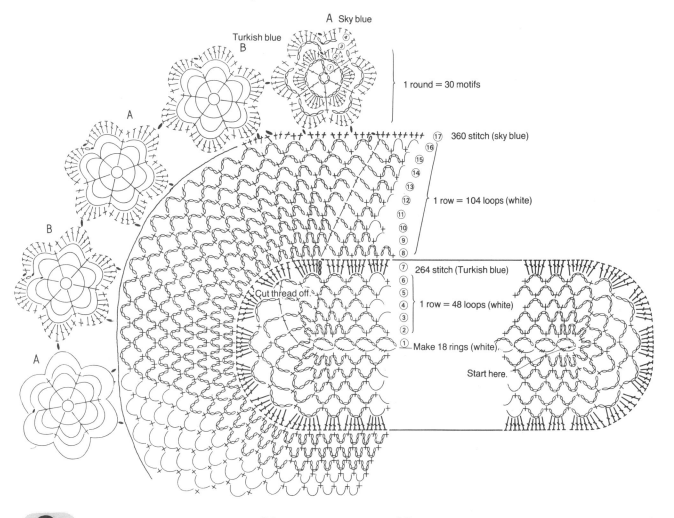

You'll need:
Crochet cotton DMC No. 40, 10g cream (437)
Steel crochet hook:
Crochet hook (0.90mm)
Finished size:
20 cm in diameter.
Instructions:
Row 1: Make ch-8 to form ring and 16-sc in ring. Row 2: Work ch-3, "ch-1, 1-dc" 15 times, ch-1, sl st at the end. Rows 3 – 4: Make square mesh working dc in ch of previous row. Row 5: Work around with dc. Rows 6 – 7: Work square mesh. Row 8: Work around with dc. Rows 9 – 12: Work square mesh increasing ch between dc. Rows 13 – 20: Work 8 patterns. Row 21: Ch-3 and repeat "ch-10, 1-dc" around. Row 22: Work around with sc and sl st-picot with 5-ch. Chart on page 81.

Basic Crochet Stitches and Symbols

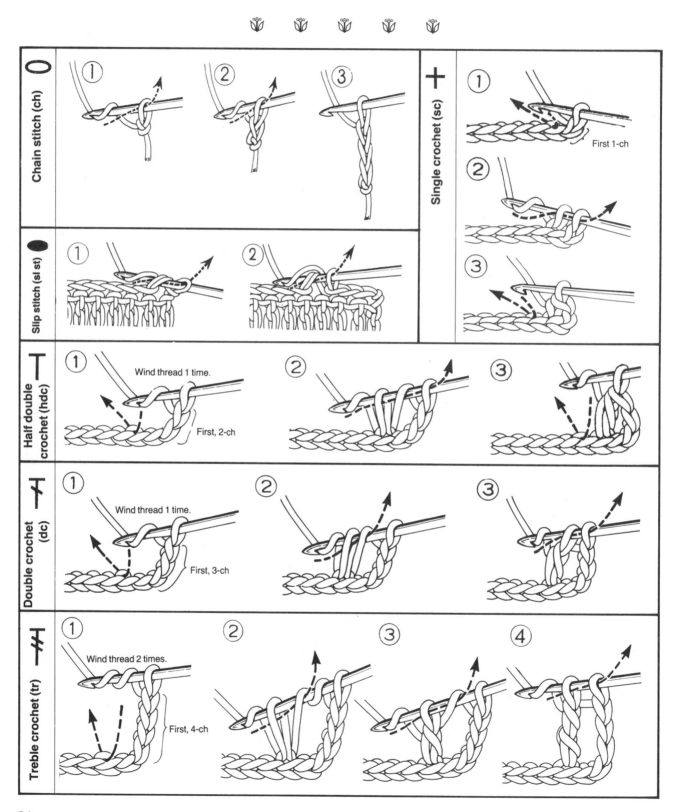

Chain stitch (ch) ⭕	① ② ③	
Slip stitch (sl st) ⬤	① ②	**Single crochet (sc)** ✛ — ① First 1-ch ② ③
Half double crochet (hdc) ⊤	① Wind thread 1 time. First, 2-ch ② ③	
Double crochet (dc) ⊤̸	① Wind thread 1 time. First, 3-ch ② ③	
Treble crochet (tr) ⧸⧸	① Wind thread 2 times. First, 4-ch ② ③ ④	

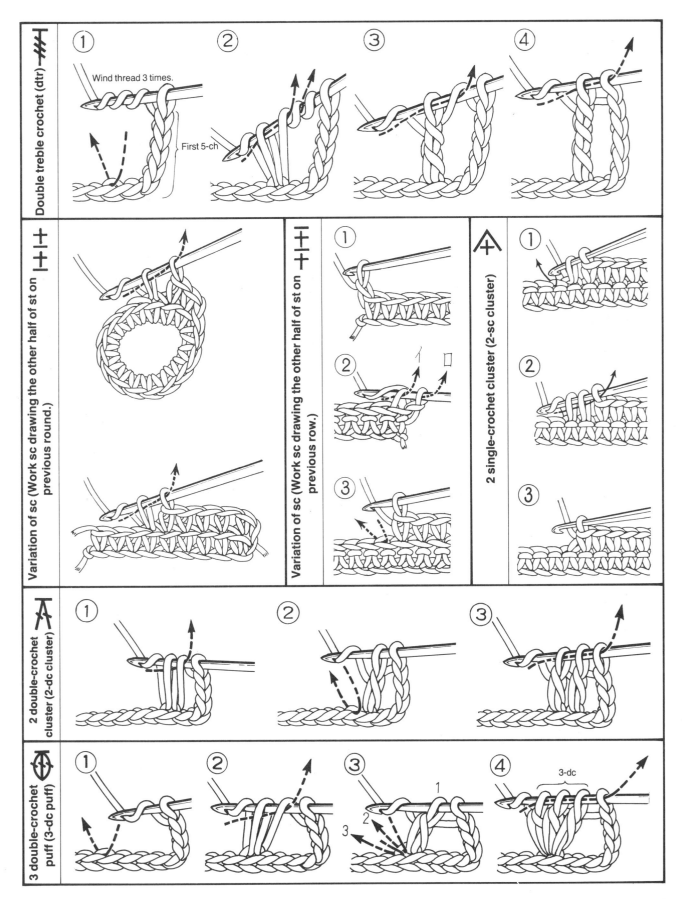

Double treble crochet (dtr)

① Wind thread 3 times. First 5-ch

②

③

④

Variation of sc (Work sc drawing the other half of st on previous round.)

Variation of sc (Work sc drawing the other half of st on previous row.)

①

②

③

2 single-crochet cluster (2-sc cluster)

①

②

③

2 double-crochet cluster (2-dc cluster)

①

②

③

3 double-crochet puff (3-dc puff)

①

②

③ 1 2 3

④ 3-dc

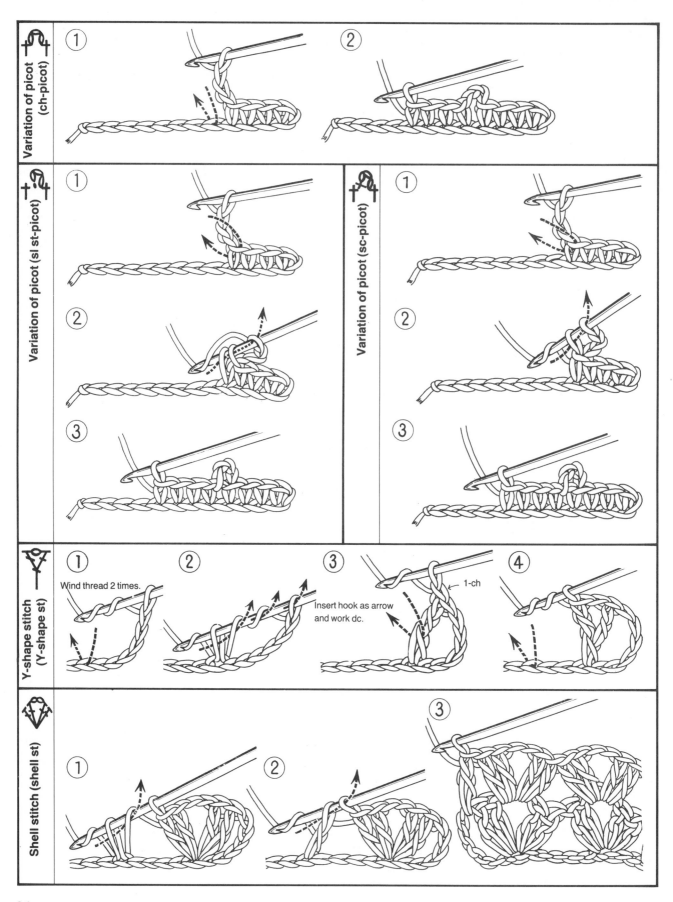

Variation of picot (ch-picot)

① ②

Variation of picot (sl st-picot)

① ② ③

Variation of picot (sc-picot)

① ② ③

Y-shape stitch (Y-shape st)

① Wind thread 2 times. ② ③ 1-ch
Insert hook as arrow and work dc. ④

Shell stitch (shell st)

① ② ③

86

Joining motifs

(1) Join together working last row of motif.

A. Sl st and sc joining
From 2nd motif, join together with completed 1st motif on last row. As in this example, work ch until joining point, insert hook in 1st motif, draw up at arrow, and work sc. Work ch and continue the last row of 2nd motif.

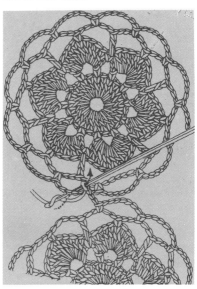

B. Picot joining
For motifs with picot on last row, join together at each top of picot. Using 3-ch picot as example, work ch-1, insert hook in picot of other piece, draw thread through and work sc. Counting this sc as 1-ch, work ch-1 to finish picot.

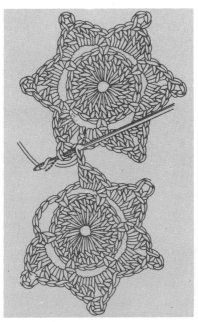

(2) Joining together after completing each motif

A. Overcasting
Place completed motifs in line and overcast every edged stitch of motif.

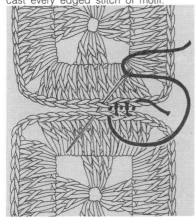

B. Net st joining
Work ch and sc making extra row between motifs.

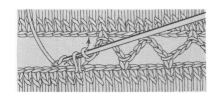

C. Replacing hook
Replace hook after working st until joining picot on last row of 2nd motif. Insert hook in st of 1st motif and draw up dropped st at arrow. Continue the last row of 2nd motif.

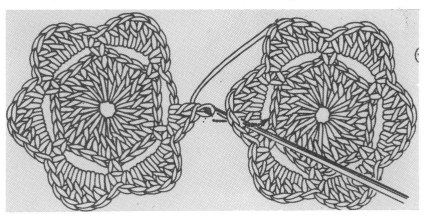

Now, you have enjoyed the patient work of your crochet, but there is one more step: Finishing perfects your work and makes each stitch neater. Here are some simple and easy methods.

Choose the one you think best based on its application to your pattern, the condition of your work, and your own working style.

A. If Your Crochet Is Beautifully Finished

If your work is clean and the stitches are neat, iron it immediately because the more the lace is washed, the more it is whitened, but the more it loses its gloss. Use sharp, rustless pins and a soft padded-surface ironing board to prevent damage to stitches.

① Place a transparent vinyl over the board on which the guidelines are drawn.

How to draw guidelines:

First, mark the center of a circle, and draw a circle according to the finished size. Divide radius into 3-5 parts and draw inner circles depending on the size of the work. Then, draw division lines according to the number of patterns made radially. For example, if there are 6 patterns around, draw 6 division lines. The more guidelines there are, the more neatly the work will be finished. However, sometimes it may become difficult to identify the stress on a pattern. Therefore, you have to decide how many lines to draw based on the characteristics of the work.

② Turn the work over and put it on the guideline board. First, pin at the center. To divide the pattern evenly, pin the work according to the guideline, pulling carefully. Pay attention to design, such as straight or curved lines. When the work is evenly stretched, remove the center pin before ironing.

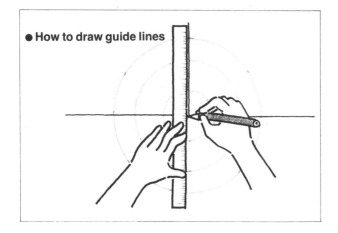

● **How to draw guide lines**

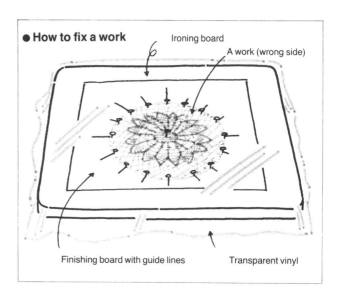

● **How to fix a work**

Ironing board

A work (wrong side)

Finishing board with guide lines

Transparent vinyl

③ If you like a soft finish, spray water over the work and adjust the warp of stitches and the shape of picot or net. The order of work in this case is from large to small, such as whole to parts, parts to details and details to stitches. If you prefer a hard finish, apply starch. A spray starch is convenient, but before using the sprayer, check to see if there is any rust on the nozzle, or any other problem in spraying.

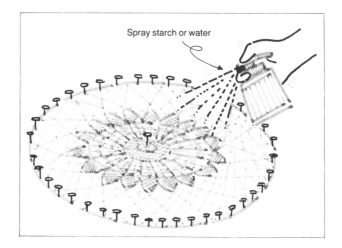

Spray starch or water

④ Apply a cover cloth. Press it from above with an iron set at high temperature to dry and fix stitches. Be careful not to burn the work. If you move the iron, it may make stitches uneven and pins will have no effect. Remove pins after the work is completely dry.

The finished sizes of doilies and centerpieces indicated here are those sizes measured after they are stretched and fixed in finishing. Therefore, the crocheted size is smaller than the finished size.

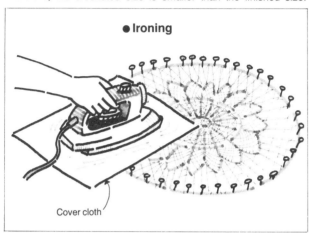

● Ironing

Cover cloth

B. If There Are Unwanted Gathers or If the Crochet Turns Inside Out

When there are puckers or the work turns inside out because of uneven stitches, finish it in the same manner as a neatly worked crochet. Pin it closely. If stitches are short in length compared with width, they can cause puckers or gathers. In such case, try to enlarge the completed work. If stitches are long in length compared with width, the work begins to turn inside out.
In this case, try to stretch the width of the work.

C. If The Work Is Soiled

Cleanliness is the essence of crochet lace, so wash the work if it is dirty. To do this, follow these steps:

① Dissolve neutral detergent in tepid water. Wash the crochet lace, shaking it or squeezing it lightly. Rinse the piece repeatedly until the water becomes clear, then wrap it in a towel to dry.
② Since all crochet cotton contains some starch, apply more starch after washing to restore its finish.
③ Put a finishing board on the ironing board. Place a vinyl over it, turn the work over on it, and pin it in the same manner as for a neatly worked crochet. Since crochet thread is cotton, it shrinks when it is washed. Individual stitches and the whole piece will look stiff and shrunken. Therefore, fix the center tightly and pin it, pulling strongly outward.
④ Dry it in an airy place. When it is 80-percent dry, put a cover cloth over it and iron by just pressing over the cloth. Be careful not to move the iron over the fabric. Remove the pins after the piece is completely dry.

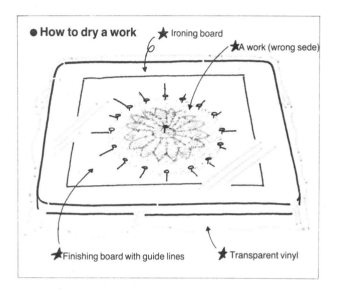

● How to dry a work — ★ Ironing board — ★A work (wrong sede)

★ Finishing board with guide lines — ★ Transparent vinyl

● **When there are stains and spots on the fabric**
In removing stains and spots, remember the quicker the better. Whenever you find stains, remove them as soon as possible.
① If it is a small stain, place the work on a towel and tap it with a cloth soaked in a soap solution. Stains will be removed easily by changing the position of the towel and tapping repeatedly.
② If stains are not pronounced they may come out just by washing; but if stains cannot be removed easily, soak the work in solution of 1 liter water and 10g neutral detergent. Stains can also be removed beautifully by boiling the piece for 10 minutes to 1 hour, depending on the stains.
③ The rest of the procedure is the same as ② – ④ of the section, "If the Work Is Soiled".

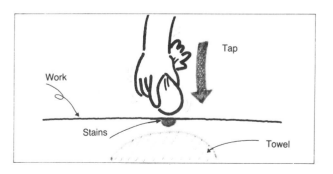

Tap

Work

Stains

Towel

D. How to Make Beautiful Frills

Here is a simple, easy method for making gorgeous frills.

① Fix a work on the ironing board as for "If Your Crochet Is Beautifully Finished" when parts of the frills are tightly stretched lengthwise.

② Apply thicker starch on the frills than on the central parts. Spray the starch in two stages, since it is difficult to dry if it is sprayed all at once.

③ When it is dry, apply a cover cloth and iron on it lengthwise. Remove pins.

④ Decide the number and position of frills according to the pattern. When frills are large, their number should be small. If frills are small in size, increase their number. Turn the fabric right-side out. Handle frills with special care. Put the thumb and index finger of the left hand on the inside part of frill positions. Hold and stretch the fabric upward and outward with the right hand, adjusting the shape with your thumb. When all frills are made, adjust outside fabric with fingertips.

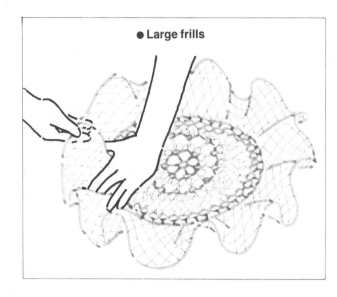

● Large frills

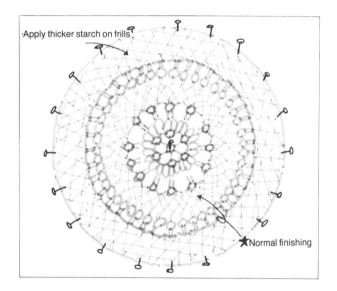

·Apply thicker starch on frills.

★ Normal finishing

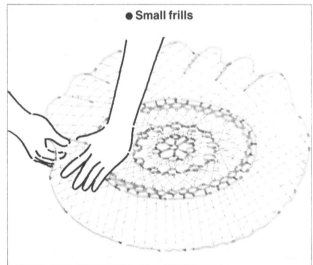

● Small frills

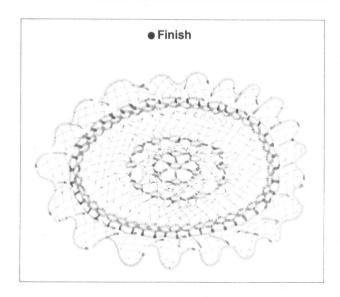

● Finish